Escaping the Housework

Front Cover:	Acer Tree.	Jan Bayliss
Back Cover	Photograph	S.Charlewood
Typesetting		B Charlewood.

ISBN 978-0-9929255-1-2

Escaping the Housework

Introduction

Poetry is more than 'the heart's speech' it is the cry of the soul.
Poetry does not depend on fashions in the world of writing, but on
the authentic voice of an individual soul, whether the poetry is set
out in verse or in prose
No-one can force their spirit into a strait jacket, any more than they
can wear shoes that are too small or the wrong shape for their feet. In
just that way no-one can be confined to a particular way of writing
which does not belong with them.
Everyone has a different, personal and clear voice and message.
The quest is to find, and to allow, that voice and that message to be
free, and then to hone the shape of what is written to the most
appropriate form for itself.
Having written poetry all my life – my first two rhyming lines were
written at the age of two – it seems, now that I am in my seventies,
time to publish some of what I have written.
I make no pretences of being a great poet - I am just a wife, mother
and grandmother, who finds the time in a busy life to scribble down a
few lines here and there, when I can escape the housework!
Some of these poems have already appeared in the following poetry
magazines:
David Allen Stringer's 'New World Creation Project';
Ian Deal's 'Image Nation', 'Bard Hair Day', 'Poet Tree' and 'The
Word';
Jennie Farley for help and advice
Dr Mrs Tulsi's 'Met-verse Muse' 'Kindred Spirit' Magazine, (as
selected by Jay Ramsay, who has been an inspiration!) 'Love Poetry'
by author.com
An Arthurian magazine, whose name I don't know!

*I thank all those, including Anna Saunders of Cheltenham, who
have encouraged me to go on writing.*

Table of Contents

1 - Going for a song

Going for a song,
my song is:
it came to me at
midnight, free;
so anyone can
have this song
from me;
it did not cost much,
just, I think,
a piece of paper
and some ink,
two minutes
of my time –I've lots
of hours saved
for a pretty song,
and so it's free –
anyone can have
this song, from me.

2003

2 - Free Verse and other forms of poems

I don't understand free verse
I've tried to do it
but I just   get worse
at every thing
its never quite the same
without a rhyme
a meter or some   foot or   other
I've tried   so hard   to cut
the mustard
and the wire
that holds
the fence
together
but all I manage is pretence
or   just   non --------sense
free verse is a dead
give – away
for me because I cannot
play
those clever games
no capital letters
for proper names
and no
punctuation
but much----------- ---- hesitation
I don't do
free
verse
because it has no rhyme or reason
and anyway I am too old and have never really tried hard enough!

2003

3 - Modern Verse

It's cheaper than Therapy -
modern poetry!

Folk write down,
as it comes,
just how they feel,
what they perceive as real:

no co-ordination needed,
convention all unheeded -

but it keeps them happy,
saves paying out for pills;

and they can rehearse
all their multifarious ills
and sell them to the likes
of you and me.

This may well help them ,
but it isn't
Poetry -
or even verse!

2004

4 - The Phoenix

(A reflection on "A Meditation on the Ancient Egyptian Text")

So, as there is but one Eternity,
I fly mad as I am!
A Phoenix on its way
upward, towards Divinity.
Burning in my wings of fire
over the generations I suspire,
aspire, from dust and ashes –
dust-particles of beauty,
microcosm of the world,
all Souls, and All-Soul;
all death and resurrection,
bird of Paradise and Hell,
of re-creation, desecration, fire.
Madness of the soul entranced am I –
the quavers and the crotchets of the lyre
Life strums to bring forth birth
this Mad Bird singing over all the Earth
changeless, forever changing –
flaming feathers ranging
over the species and the Souls
and all Beliefs and all the Names of Gods –
Phoenix of all Life, Lives' hopes,
upwards towards Divinity
mad as I am, I fly!

2003

5 - Phoenix Rising

And have you never heard
of me the myth-true bird?
Singing my song, I fly,
toward the waiting sky.
See how I now arise
from sorrow and from sighs,
from ancient, burning nest,
I rise in glowing zest!
I am all man's desire
arising from the fire:
as all Time, I am, old,
with plumage fiery gold –
immortal Life and Youth
blazing eternal Truth-
I, old age despising,
Flame-fathered phoenix, rising!

2003

6 - The Pelican

O Love! I have let you burn freely –
why do you scorch my heart?
I have allowed you a free spirit
why do you sear my soul?
I have let you spread your wings –
why do you keep me caged?

Oh Love!
I have let fall my blood to feed you –
why do you keep me starved?
I have plucked out my plumage to warm you –
why do you turn, disgusted, from my nakedness?

Winter. 1999.

7 - **November 11th**

Last spring was full of brides:
winter sees only widows….

Summer was bright with colour:
autumn knows only shadows….

Last night was full of dreams –
today has forgotten them……

Yesterday thronged with young men,
but tomorrow buries them ------

Unless the falling poppies teach us peace,
their red rain falling, like a cloud of blood,
useless the patriotic sacrifice,
and all in vain tomorrow's motherhood.

11/11/2003.

8 - Flanders

You can feel the silence,
smell the pain:
after these many years
Man's signature is here,
written in blood and fear.
No bird sings in these woods –
nothing moves,
but, blackened and bare, one tree
amongst the brambles stands,
stretched out, like Calvary -
and oh, so many christs in khaki
with no resurrection from
their cold and muddy tomb.
And it was all in vain:
lives given,
their glorious manhood spent.
Who did not know, before,
the ghastly waste of war?
Now see the poppies grow
red on green -
bright blood on a foreign flag.
And yet – we who survive,
untaught by death, we live.
Let us remember then,
their honour,
but our shame these things can be
repeated in the name
of Liberty –
Oh God!
All these Christs,
in khaki!

Belgium: 1985

9 - Iraqi Sands

Sand on the car roof.
On the foot-path too,
I'm not by the sea,
I'm far inland.
Is it the war then
that churns this crunchy
dust, that's faintly pink,
from dunes far away
If I wash it off
will it turn to ash
thrown up by tanks
and by marching feet -
blown across the sun
to fall here, today?
Is this a 'Just War'
or just a war for oil?
If I wash the sand off
will it turn to blood?

2003

10 - War in Iraq

I can wash desert sand
away with water;
but I can't wash away
so much spilt blood,
restore lost innocence.
Everyone sees this war
on television;
people blown up or burnt
before our eyes;
we cannot now pretend
it's not happening;
just like the advertisements
it's always there.
'Don't buy a paper then,
don't switch on the box!
If we're not watching
war will go away.'
It was Einstein who said
a butterfly could
cause the world to shift
if it but moved an inch;
so what if they drop bombs
of spent uranium -
how much will the earth move -
such missiles flying?
We can't bring back to life
the innocent dead;
those killed by 'friendly fire';
such a misnomer!
How can a bullet tell
who it is will die
from its unfriendly kiss
as loving as Judas.

Where are the children, too,
who used to play here –
has each one grabbed a gun
 play-fighting 'them and us'?
or are they simply dead?
Now where is the Christ
anointed, to bring life –
for this is Easter-
just tell that to the Kurds-
they have become used to gas!

Easter 2003

11 - War Widow

Her face
still, grave,
retains its grace
no muscle moves
or sigh escapes.

Her customary calm
lies over all –
no lines
mar her beauty,
no sighs –

it's still her duty
to be in command:
she betrays
no sadness,
and no fear,

just the trace
the path
on her still face,
of one single
tear.

2003

12 - Meditation at Prinknash Abbey

Mist filled the valleys lie
where gold sun-shafts,
though they touch the heights,
yet fail to light the day.
In autumn's glory, trees
hold high the veils of mist
in lifted branches:
the robin's note changes
when he sings, and herons fly.

Nature's panoply
unfolds before the eye;
while leaf mould and wood smoke
woo fragrance from thin air;
and raindrops orchestrate
symphonies of water-
rain above and underfoot
the loud spring rises
where the dead leaves lie.

Thin shifts of Autumn shroud
and beautify the scene,
tinting the distant hills
with grey haze and with blue-
smudging out the awkward,
ugly works of man..

Escaping the Housework

Upon these hills and valleys
Beauty preserves its reign:
from Stone Age until now
men have stood, wondering,
at all this Cotswold beauty:

cut but one tree, and all may fall:
remove the grass from one small,
nameless, patch, and light
may fade upon the distant brow
of that far hill, cross-hatched by sun light, even now!

November, 2002

13 - From my late Sister

'Life has been interesting!
It continues – souls immortal
do not linger by the portal
that leads to boredom and despair,
but rise upon the lambent air
to find the most important thing –
new work to do, and friends to greet,
and new acquaintances to meet.
Do not be sad for me – I'm free at last
from all the ills and trammels of the past.
Rejoice! My hard-run race is run,
and now a new experience begun,
to test my intellect and memory.
But do nor weep. For there will always be
love for those dear ones – every friend
who stayed to comfort me 'til this life's end –
tell them how much I love them still,
if I can help them, then I will help still
and one day, when they join again with me
in freedom and in spirit we again will be
a shining and a joyous company!'

SAC & MEC. (Dcd. 4th. October 2000.)

14 - Love is a river

This is the river into which
we both agreed and plunged
it now flows, full and rich
and cannot be expunged;
for while this is our life
he swims beside me
and I am his wife,
my husband he;
we, together borne
onward by the stream,
each let our lives adorn
the other's dream.
We hold each other high
so that we float -
for see, my Love and I
need no built boat
on Life's great river –
each are held aloft
by that great giver
Love, flowing between
as we both care and share,
keeping hearts fresh and green!

09/04/2005

15 - Love in Autumn

Now have the poppies lulled themselves to sleep
and Autumn's leaves are falling, golden, deep.
The swifts have flown, the robins change their call
lush creeper reddens on the crumbling wall;
cow-parsley shows bare ribs where the lane leads
and rose-bay-willow herb lets fall its seeds
like silken puffs of silver, spider-spun,
while sheaves of corn stand, golden in the sun
Now is the time when Nature gathers up
unravelled glories of her summer cup;
blue smoke of bon-fires shows where leaves and weeds
are burnt to make a place for next year's seeds
planting anew Spring's fragile, wondrous stock
of primrose, violet and lady's smock;
while, in between, cold Winter lowers its head
the tasselled poppies slumber in their bed.
Now is the time to hoard Love's treasures rare,
with hugs and kisses warm the chilly air:
so with the flagrant poppies we'll retire
to charm dull Winter with our sweet desire!

07/10/2004

16 - Loss

You see, it's never lost to love;
never wasted - always learning
is found where Love's at work,
where consolation's offered.
Love's pain is close to ecstasy
because it's grown from love.
Love does not die, it only changes –
passion to knowledge,
which transmutes into concern.
Nor does it matter if we
are not loved in return
since Love itself is one,
whole and complete.
Offered, Love cannot be divided
and cannot be destroyed;
yet Love may be stored –
may be laid safe away
almost forgotten; until one day
something is heard or seen
or thought – Love's whole again
as bright as that first day
how long ago? Not long
in our eternal scheme of things.
So many loves in life
Each whole and perfect,
each shining bright
because it is a given gift
the gift of all Soul's light!

July, 2011

17 - This is Love

This is love that will transcend
the love of flesh and blood,
it is the love
that holy spirits send
for all our good.
The love that learns
to leave the flesh behind
and rise above
mundane things of this world,
and of this life,
where none perfection find.
And we must learn
acceptance of the best
that we are offered –
We must learn Love.

2013

18 - The Marriage of Minds

There is a marriage of the minds
that lovers make, and friends can also take –
a synthesis of thoughts
and of the song that winds
as tangle in the lake
moves with the draft of water
through the weir; so this love
surges between the souls
and floods their being
so each sees what the other's seeing -
and understands the sight
turning pain to joy again, and light.,
because they're understood.

Such love
needs no divorce proceedings
since it is based on love
much deeper than the love of flesh and bone,
that breeds contention,
and, of course, dissention,
likewise, the loss of that sweet freedom
that is Love's greatest gift:
in spirits' loving there is no such rift.
 No one is ever left sad and alone
deep in dissatisfaction.

This is the height and depth of Love
that's felt when two souls meet,
and recognizing, greet
a soul that is a part
of that great family, that league of Art,
of Poetry and music – loving minds
that flock together in the winds
of that sweet Communion
in mystic union with every soul
that truly thinks,
and therefore truly lives!

2003

19 - Friendship and Love

There is a kind of Love that silent stays,
that yearns on the beloved, sighs, and prays
only for what is good and right
to be around the loved ones, in their sight.

So is my love for all my dearest friends
who gather round me – not for ends
of their own wishing: so my open heart
allows them, when they will, to enter or depart.

And it is this that brings the healing bliss
of Love, for everything that lives, and is.
Are you troubled? Then my love will soothe
your heart, and make your pathway smooth.

Are you grieving? Then comforting Love
will fly from me to you, as birds above
fly quickly to their hungry, crying young
to feed them, and then sing their sweetest song.
Are you lonely? Then my love will gently bring
another soul to company your sad soul's spring.

This is not love as by the world beheld,
debased and cheapened, spirit all withheld
but clean and fresh, and pure affection, mine,
that will not see the souls I love repine.

Come, rest upon the solace I extend –
in friendship's name my heart I lend
to comfort, solace and accompany –
what ever you might wish, that will I be.

No hardened marble dwells within my breast,
for I can laugh or sorrow, with the rest:
can bring you joy and simple fun
in dreary torrent or in warming sun –
true Friendship lives to serve, and serves to live,
and ever pure and simple Love will give.

2012

20 - Regret

My cheek cannot remember
the warm curve of your shoulder;
your hand would not know my body, older,
drooping breast, sagging belly, rippled thigh –
this thing, no longer beautiful, is not the I
your body knew so well.
but it has borne the swell of all your children.
Now that *that* love is dead
that used to pillow safe my sleeping head,
hands straying to my breast
to find their comfortable rest
until the morning.
Now I am mourning:
my cheek is damp with tears
no longer with your sweat
from our sweet loving
that love has gone, long gone
to my long regret,
regretful longing.

May 2014

21 - Voyager 1937

My life is a boat with no compass;
a vessel with no anchor;
a ship with no sail.
For there is no remaining purpose,
nothing to strive for –
no aim in which I may prevail.
My heart was boarded by pirates
buccaneers stole my thoughts,
privateers my words.
I lurch towards safe water,
skimming the lights
among the common herds.
I claim my rights –
declaring for a new charter
of what my life should be,
and what my destination –
I seek for love and laughter
to give new hope –
not resignation –
Victory!

March 1996. When diagnosed with breast cancer

22 - Inspired by Jay Ramsay

And your words have put me in mind
of those days, now so long ago,
when I trod green ways that wind
through wild woods, to the lake below;
there some precious days of girlhood
were passed in hours of pure delight
in the shadow of the wildwood
watching the damsel flies' blue flight.
Mother Ireland! County Sligo!
Could I but be there once again
hearing all the streams' soft prattle,
gentle splashing of the rain;
feel once more the whispered hush
of breathing trees and water-rush;
the long-drawn heart-held-still of days
that dawned and closed in leafy haze.
So I travel back in spirit,
finding, in a certain measure
where far-off, but remembered still
the lagan was receiving treasure
from the stream's out-pouring spill,
I went, bird –sung, insect-haunted
along beside the water glade –
how merrily my young self jaunted
through the boreen's green-gold shade!

2003

23 - The Boreen

I remember deep lanes, shady.
that lie by water meadows lush
where the flies makes music lazy
in afternoon's gold, sleepy hush
I have wandered in my thoughts there,
have trod the sunken lane along,
watched the dragonflies that hover,
above the tangled meadow weeds,
I have dreamed of walking over
fields waist deep in dew-damp reeds
where the fairy-scattered iris
rise from hidden water-ways,
blazing, golden, through the days.
Ah! When my soul is free once more,
I'll go again to tramp the boreen
leading to the lough's cool shore,
I will hear the songbird's sorrow,
disturbed and frantic, as I pass,
hear as brindled cows crop grass.
Then I'll seek the deep green pathway
with all the damsel flies afloat,
see the massing of the mayflies –
and there my yearning soul will gloat
over treasure none can purchase-
but where the spirit, free, can float.

 2003

A 'Boreen' is a narrow Irish sunken lane un-surfaced, except by
moss, usually over-hung by trees, and leading down to a lake, or
'lough'.
A boreen is a place where one might expect anything to
happen……………

24 - Faery Land

As you stroll down the boreen,
beware, on your left hand,
a faery maiden can be seen
spinning gold from sand.

As you go down the boreen,
look, for on your right side
a Gentle girl is weaving
linen from the tide;

she weaves a shawl of fern leaves
trimmed with threads of gold
if you should spy the thread she weaves,
you're hers, to have and hold!

As you stroll to the water
toward the blue lough's strand
King Lir's favourite daughter
will beckon with her hand –

'tis you will soon be grieving,
if you touch that slender hand
if you espy the weaving,
or see the spinning sand!

2004

25 - Summer Storm

Clouds gathered;
moving, they darkened
purple in their greyness
overhead.
At last the steady fall
of rod-straight rain
surrounded all;
the atmosphere
heavy and hot
in spite of being wet.
So, no quenching of the heat
as drops fell: just humidity.
Then came wet and rich the scent –
unmistakably - of rain,
so flower-fresh,
fragranceing the afternoon -
and, just as suddenly, it stopped:
stones dried at once,
and all was still again,
birds silenced:
none dared fly.
Heat: and every flower-pot
miraculously dry!

2004

26 - Floods

To start at the beginning,
they need shelter.
To start at the beginning,
they need food.
Starting at the beginning,
they need warmth.

Where, then, can we hope to start.
How can we help them, give them hope,
comfort them
when they have seen their homes drowning.
herds drowning.
In England –
where there is always safety,
in England, where these things do not happen?

To start at the beginning
the floods have happened!

People go, grey-faced, on their way
in their waders, or small boats –
and all the National News today
is filled with sad, tired quotes
as folk struggle for their life.
Today they need us all to know
their mutual ruin is rife.

How can they ever start their lives again,
and face such desolation?
We need to share the misery and pain
of this dark inundation.

Where the willing hands for all?
Women with urns of tea
served up in some chilly old school hall
where, wet and cold, folk flee –
all their possessions gone in mud and rain ?

How can they start their lives again,
how re-make their lives, forget the hurt
so such a drowning pain
Starting at the beginning,
how shall we, and these, our countrymen,
save their lives and our ancient treasures
from rotting detritus and decay.

Starting at the beginning
There Were No Measures
Put In Place
for this painful rain,
This cruel inundation!

Winter, 2000-2001

27 - Tsunami

This is Gaia, goddess who can show
love and horror to both beast and man;
can shake the seas awake, and make them rise
swelling to swallow in their furious path
all creatures, and all things upon the Earth.
This is the Mother Goddess, whom we wound
with daily crimes against her sanctity,
seeking to rob her richest veins of ore
greedy as children who, in infancy
grab at their mother's breast and cry for more.

This is Gaia, whom we should not harm,
whose laws are best to keep and not to shun,
whose might can answer all our puny strength,
in ways we cannot even start to know.

Let us not cry that God looked not on us
it's Mother Gaia who will always do
whatever she, the Earth Herself, decides,
whose every whim humanity must bide –
earthquake and storm, volcano, tsunami wave –
still we must suffer what our Earth provides –
we can but patch and heal that which we see
for She is greater than we'll ever be,
and what we do, however bold our task
we are but helpless in Her mighty grasp!

January 2005

28 - Millennium 2000

Here we stand; it was to be
so very special: they said to me
"Millennium! Great! All things made anew
I rather thought them too
optimistic too enthralled in thought
of what "2000" meant – what has it brought?

Man still has not changed his mind
the deaf still cannot hear, the blind still blind
The scientists make harsher, stronger 'arms'
and animals still suffer on intensive farms.

Upon the edge of the Millennium, what's new?
Lies are still lies and truth still true
Nothing has changed because a clock ticks on-
and much of what was beautiful is gone.

In any case – because the time
we tell by changes, clime to clime –
what is "Two thousand" for European man
is not " two thousand" in Egypt or Japan!

And if it was, what difference would it make?
Our politicians still make promises to break!
Our wisest men are still a ship of fools,
and no one teaches Beauty in our schools;
come, brothers, sisters! Let us raise the cry –
let us try to change it, so that none shall die
in combat, conflict, hunger, cold –
let's make a difference before this year is old!

2000

29 - Solstice

Soon will come Solstice,
then the year will change;
the days will turn around,
and new aims will be found,
life rearrange
to its long promise,
all will begin anew -
be you the serpent then,
to cast your out-worn skin,
your Golden Age anew begin.

For see, each new snakeskin
is made from deep within
the serpent's own resources;
so too must we, from deep inside -
inside our hearts and brains,
inside our burning souls,
create the garments our souls weave and wear
with thoughts, words and feelings,
even if we grieve.

We must our own sharp critics be -
all that is not fair and good
remove, lest it stain the soul,
rotting the deep heart-wood
of all our stalwart trees.
Care for each other, then, must be a part,
for all that we must jettison
some bliss that we would dream on!

Beside that golden gate
of Truth, of Poetry,
that only poets' minds can see –
Soon will come Solstice,
then the year will change –
the days will turn around!

June 2000

30 - Violets

The grass is cut. My violets felled.
They were purple, fragile, fair,
I knew the mower spelled
their downfall, and my small despair.
They were beautiful, as yet un-seeded-
so next year, none will grow.

A sad thing, not to have their scent
rise to my window, fragrant,
delicate as old silk or gloves
of soft leather; leaving the flagrant
wall-flowers that he loves,
who cut the grass, and felled my violets.

2012

31 - Shared Harvest

A bird in the laburnum tree
sings the whole day, cheerily.
And well might he be gay and merry -
my good-man tends all kinds of berry;
and since we use no poisoned pill
for insects, he can eat his fill
of currants, raspberry, strawberry –
there's quite enough to share with me
the fruits that Nature gives to us;
And yet he makes a birdlike fuss
if he should just spy one of us
gathering fruits! – But we will share
Earth's bounty, as he scolds us there!

July. 2000

32 - Hand

One leaf, flushed by autumn:
like a pink palm, held out
in silent supplication
for one more day upon the vine,
begging for shelter from the storm,
that will finally detach it
from the parent plant, to flutter
to the earth, where it will rot.

Wind rises, the long nights grow chill;
only the russet chestnuts
glow, glorious, along the path,
safe from the marauding winds,
half hidden in the mossy grass,
like jewels, for small boys to find.

I am touched by that small, pink hand,
would like to save its delicate tint
and construction, for a while |:
too late! The summer spell is broken
and all the leaves must fall.

October 2004

33 - Haikus for Spring

1. In the spiky grass,
   braving frost and icy winds,
   golden aconites.

2. Movement of green buds
   thrusting their way through cold earth,
   Spring flowers rising.

3. Gently the seed falls
   dropping on to the soft ground
   bearing more tree-life.

4. Drops from the willow
   spill into lake water
   refreshing its flow.

5. Gossamer silk webs
   crossing the spring grass
   with droplets and spiderlings.

6. Strawberry leaves
   white with starry flowers
   this summer's fruit.

1998

34 - Haikus for Summer

1. Here open daisies,
   glowing in the sun,
   reflecting back light.

2. Ripening seed-corn
   glowing in the sun
   loaves in the making

3. Moving like a queen
   between the ridges of corn
   Persephone comes.

4. Last call of the thrush
   swallows departing;
   we await winter.

5. Strawberry leaves
   dead and brown on the ground
   last summer's fruit

1991

35 - Tankas for the Seasons

Spring.

1 .In the green water
   frogspawn, like gleaming jelly
   gathers round the stems
   of the tall irises;
   froglets, and food for fishes!

2 .Small birds building nests;
   hidden in hawthorn thickets
   will lay bright blue eggs –
   hatching young birds, to call,
   and to sing all next summer.

3. Clutch of sky blue eggs,
   cradled softly in the nest,
   hen robin sits tight,
   hatching new life among dead twigs;
   feathers will warm young birds.

4. Arise, beloved,
   come into the spring garden
   to see the flowers
   growing from last years seedpods –
   promises of summer sun!

Summer.

1. In the golden fields
   men and women with strong arms
   gather the golden grain,
   bring the harvest back home,
   food for the coming year!

Autumn.

1. Mist of Autumn fires
   drifting over hillsides,
   burning of old leaves;
   we make all safe and tidy:
   prepared for the next spring.

2. Tall poppies standing
   strongly on the verdant fields,
   bright and red as blood,
   growing where young men,
   fallen, give back life from their bones

All the above, Haikus and Tankas, were written under the influence of Jenny Farley, a wonderful teacher! SAC.

1998

36 - For a School Friend

A shady bank, sun-warmed,
'midst springing thyme in bloom,
rose-shaded over-head,
a singing stream below,
with music, sweetest music, too,
to lift the heart and mind
to higher thoughts; just here
with some friend, tried and dear,
to share the feast of song –
what more could heart desire,
soul long for, spirit seek?
Such is the stuff of dreams-
ephemeral but sweet!

Written for Brian my friend of many years, who loves music as much
or even more, than I do!

37 - Castel Y Bere

The sea was here – gone now,
it has forever ebbed -
yet still the sea-birds flock
in thousands to this rock,
beside the castle wall;
on grassland, hear them call
as if on water still.
The castle walls rise, sheer:
doors open to thin air;
steps of a broken stair
where once the sea-gate was,
lead now to only grass .
Long dead Welsh Princes!
This in your prime, was home,
safe strong-hold ,too;
now stark in desertion,
but unbowed and undefeated,
here its ruined bide -
and could yet serve again,
should time but turn the tide!

1995

The ruined, beautiful, castle of Owen Glendower, which was once
close to the sea shore, stands land locked below Cader Idris.

38 - Abbey House Gardens

This tranquil place,
where grow the lily and the rose,
lush-lawned, box-formed;
whispered by waters
sweet with scented phlox,
candled around with hollyhocks,
confines within it Beauty's resting place:
A gentle garden, green, and full of grace,
that offers shade and sunlight,
light and dark; pleached pears,
and cordoned apples, gillie-flowers.
Here is the place to pass some summer hours
to hear the buzz of bees, the water's song,
beside the yew-hedge and the ancient stone.
Such beauty: such a scented Paradise
within the bounds of this old Abbey lies –
no wonder then, that in this Eden,
Adam and Eve, in innocent undress,
tend to the flowers, and sculpt the wilderness!

The Abbey House Gardens, Malmesbury
2004 August

39 - Sea Scape with Rocks

The sea laps at our feet,
grey, green, mysterious:
too deep to swim or wade;
above us rise the cliffs:
too steep to scale or climb –
yet we must go on.
We may not stop or stay
by night we must be gone
and time runs on.
This sheer wall of stone
beside us gives no room
for anyone to pass –
no room for other
travellers at all;
and both of us
are height-sick,
suffering vertigo:
still we must go on.
Far out to sea a ship
is passing by,
"dressed over all"
I think they say,
as if to honour
June's farewell to May.
We remain afraid;
but must drive on.
no head for heights,
mother or daughter!

Our laughter
and our jokes
just meant to hide
how nervous both are:-
we must neither see
the cliffs above us,
nor, below, the sea!

With my daughter, Jocelynne, at Lynmouth, May/June, 2003

40 - The Royal Forest of Dean

Above each hill the buzzard flies,
from every bush the nuthatch cries,
fresh forest-greenness scents the air,
beauty is present everywhere.
In hidden dells the running stream,
where children laugh and poets dream,
shines sudden, a bright silver thread ;
with wildflowers all around it spread;
on tree-clad slope and high green hill
enclosed, where sheep stand sentinel.
King Charles, the second of that name,
decreed amends to Cromwell's shame-
who felled the trees and made all sad –
the Foresters, for Restoration glad,
planted an oak, in his Good Memory –
 it stands, a great and mighty tree
guarding in this cherished place,
two thousand years of history and grace.

For Wendy and Douglas, Autumn, 2002

41 - Glencoe

I heard the sound of keening
as we travelled through Glencoe
I knew its heart-rent meaning,
and my own heart filled with woe
for the long-dead women keening
their dead, of long ago.
I stood quite still, and leaning,
along the mountainside
with my heart so full of sorrow -
and yet with a strange pride.

The sound had stirred reaction
in the echoes of my heart,
for that ancient, cruel action
is still somehow a part
of the fibre of my being –
though I've left that haunted Glen,
I will take with me always
the 'seeing' I had then.

Oh sad MacDonald women!
I hear you keen and weep,
through the reaches of the midnight
in my useless search for sleep.

I heard the sound of keening,
as we travelled through Glencoe,
and I still mourn for those women
who suffered long ago
in that place called 'Glen of Weeping'
for that murder, in Glencoe.

1990

42 - Old Age

So, this is Peace!
Youth's fires are now a gentle glow;
one does not strive for mere appearances,
it is much better far to stay, than go
contentment this!
The world can pass us by
without ambition tearing at the heart
the centre is no longer 'Me' and 'My'
but resignation, dignified:
for things not done will not be now:
no matter, for the time is sweet,
and light is kinder, when the logs burn low!

1985

43 - Identity Crisis

I have watched you swim
in an ocean of adulation
seeking for identity
in what you hope is admiration:
for what have you that anyone can see
that makes you what you wish to be?

This is how it is with all of us:
we come into the world alone
and leave with nothing but the omnibus
edition of the love that we have won.

Watching, and seeing your great need
I cannot help but love you –
for what you are, and what you'd like to be;
for what you wish that other folk could see.
And if those things you'll never be,
I will still love you!

44 - Portrait of Mary Shelly

Your high, pale forehead framed by hair
hanging in ringlets, silky, fair,
bright golden brown, and hanging down
below the shapely shoulders, white.
Your face, half smiling, seeming calm,
whilst inside must have been alarm
at your life-long predicament –
the family feuds that meant
you had to earn life by your pen.
And where was your beloved then?
That inkstand on your desk – the pen –
I've seen before, and they were his
whose life you shared – and what is this
in your locket on a chain?
his miniature, without a doubt:
the face of Shelley, yet again.
And ah! Yours is a lovely face
but in those clear eyes is the trace
of sadness, settled, and unending;
yet with the peace of faith transcending
because you knew that when you fled
this world, reunion with your dead
would compensate your life of sadness –
certain of eternal gladness.
Mary! You suffered for the Art,
ideals, of One who held your heart,
while, in a casket, you held his,
and dreamed of an eternal bliss!
2001

45 - The Singing Heart

And Mary said her husband's heart
upon her desk still throbbed and sang;
and still, when singers start to sing,
and when a poet plies his art,
his shrill, gold, voice again will ring.

And how that heart will throb and glow
with a joyous beat to know
that still a voice is lifted so,
and like the skylark rises, leaps,
thrilling the all-surrounding air
in spite of pain and love's despair -
speaks from the unfathomable deeps
of feeling only poets know,
and writes on, in humility
as did his antecedent Bard –
his Mentor from eternity!

Wear then the mantle gentle Friend,
of him whose poetry you love,
and wear it until your life's end,
and know yourself blessed from above.
Shine as his heart shines, lambently,
with beauty and true poetry.
Be unafraid, the Muse is still
beside you, shining on your art,
with the bright beams of Shelley's heart!

Written in 1999, for Jay Ramsay, Poet, who also loves Shelly

46 - Lady of the Lake

Three times five hundred years
deep in my watery home,
I've lived so full of tears,
dwelling beneath the foam
flowing from mountain stream;
I guard the Sword of Light
that once great Arthur wore.
Thus, when the time is right,
I will produce once more
sword, scabbard, to be worn
by chosen warrior–king;
oaths that were once forsworn,
with great shame lingering,
shall have cause not to mourn.
Swift the hour passes
like wind's deep mystery
over fresh grasses,
and then shall History
turn all the time around –
find the chosen Bearer
who will wear Arthur's sword
flame Truth forever!

2005

47 - Summer school - creative writing

Women,
writing,
dreaming on pages.
sisters in dreams.
Women,
all ages,
backgrounds,
putting on pages
separate themes.
Women,
all eager,
writing on pages,
imagined stories:
women's dreams.

With thanks to Jenny Farley.

48 - Light on Leckhampton Hill

Now night fades from the sky:
the birds sing louder yet;
dew spangles, on the grass
spiders sit, spinning nets
to catch the drops of dream ends,
in the west the moon descends:
all the bright stars have flown.

Now the pearl-grey morning
drifts soft across the lawn –
day's colours start to glow –
the sun will shortly show
dawn light above the hill –
day opens like a rose
unfurling, ray by ray,
as petals open up,
to fill the morning cup
of beauty in still light –
another perfect dawn.

2004-08-27

49 - Flamenco

Raucous and caustic,
Flamenco singers
howl and tap their heels,
shouting the basic
instincts of mankind –
sexual need and war,
yearning for women
or a burning Cause;
drumming and stamping
out a song that bores
to the visceral depths
of all our natures;
snapping fingers at
all the conventions,
and yet containing
all their emotions
into song and dance.
A woman's skirt whirls,
clicking castanets,
incite, and yet repel
the man she yearns for,
knows she cannot have –
conventions still hold,
though she is aflame.
Rhythm of heart-beat
grows faster as the heart
beats to her desire;
yet her dance and song
tire her beyond hope
of consummation –
sad and common fate
of all humankind!
2002

50 - Twelve eggs for cream

Sweet memories that haunt me:
cool, stone-floored kitchen,
old range, hooks for bacon,
ancient meat –jack in the chimney;
sago in the cupboard
and two butler's baskets;
screen for the garden door -
too torn to stop the daft.
Rows of measuring jugs,
'Indian Bird' plates ranged
on the Welsh dresser shelves.
In the tiled front hall hung
heads of defunct buffalo
stuffed and horned round the wall.

On the stairs' turn, a grandfather clock
that once struck thirteen times
and struck my mother cold!
House I can't return to -
another owns it now;
he's taken down my swing
dug up the privet hedge
that once saved my young life.
Stable and tack room gone -
Housing on the orchard,
and both old wells filled in.

Escaping the Housework

In winter, those few men
left in the village were called
to dig sheep from the snow
that lay on Bredon Hill –
We dug the snow out too,
around the house, to where
the bath room was to be-
when the plumbing man returned
from war, to make the door .
Most I remember green-
deep green of orchard grass
studded with daffodils.
below the apple, pear, and plum.

Owls hooting in the yews
that fringed the cottage lawn,
roses, and lupin trees
popping their seeds out – ping!
There was my 'Wendy' house
built near the hens I loved:
Hens in the orchard too,
penned behind fox-proof wire,
sleeping in raised up huts,
steep slides led down with rungs
placed across to stop claws
slipping as they dashed down
to the long trough for food;
as the hens were gobbling
I would be nest egg robbing
eggs for baking, breakfast -
I could swap twelve eggs for cream,
fresh from the farmer's dairy.
Cream! A change from custard
with Sunday's apple pie!

Escaping the Housework

Autumn fruit: gooseberries,
plums from lower branches –
the ladder forbidden
to little girls like me –
fruit laid with care in sieves
sewn over well with sacking,
then taken to the train
by Snowball, in the trap,
bound for the jam factory.
Apples were stored in my room,
their scent deeply absorbed
into the panelling.
My room was bird-song lulled,
orchard blossom scented -
Ah! Sweet dreams from youth:
Twelve eggs for cream!

07/07/2014

Sylvia Charlewood is a wife, mother, and grandmother who has written poetry all her life. In her seventieth decade, she has decided to make a selection to offer to others. Her poems are simple and usually refer to the small, daily happenings in life. Her great love is for the work of P B Shelley, whose wonderful lyrical poetry has inspired her since she was a young child.

This is the first selection; others will be on their way.

www.ingramcontent.com/pod-product-compliance
Lightning Source LLC
Chambersburg PA
CBHW071851020426

42331CB00007B/1961